# THE

# BANANA

# COOKBOOK

## 50 SIMPLE AND DELICIOUS RECIPES

SAM BROOKS

summersdale

An Hachette UK Company
www.hachette.co.uk

Summersdale Publishers Ltd
Part of Octopus Publishing Group Limited
Carmelite House
50 Victoria Embankment
LONDON
EC4Y 0DZ
UK

www.summersdale.com

Printed and bound in China

ISBN: 978-1-78685-983-9

Substantial discounts on bulk quantities of Summersdale books are available to corporations, professional associations and other organisations. For details contact general enquiries: telephone: +44 (0) 1243 771107 or email: enquiries@summersdale.com.

# CONTENTS

# INTRODUCTION

There's more to the banana than meets the eye. They're well known for being delicious snacks to enjoy on their own and are full of energy, to fuel us through the day, and potassium, for a healthy heart.

But did you know that they're also great team players? Their unique nutritional make-up means they can be used in recipes as a substitute for fats, such as butter. They can also take the place of eggs and sugar in snacks, desserts and smoothies, and they add moisture and texture to breads and cakes. Most of all, they impart that distinctive, sweet banana flavour that complements so many other foods and makes your dishes delicious.

This handy book brings you a selection of the best banana recipes, both traditional and new. Whether you like to eat your bananas hot or cold, whether you're looking for drinks, breakfast foods, tasty snacks, or a show-stopping dessert, within these pages are a range of simple recipes to inspire you, satisfy you, and celebrate this humble yellow fruit.

Welcome to *The Banana Cookbook*!

# KITCHEN ESSENTIALS

Before you start baking, it's useful to know what equipment you'll need. The list below is a good indicator of what is required for most of the recipes in this book.

 **Baking paper** – This is essential for lining tins and trays to make sure your cakes don't stick.

 **Baking trays/tins** – The ones you will need for this book are a deep 20-cm square tray, a 20-cm square tin, a 20-cm round springform tin, a 12-hole muffin tin, a 17 x 9 x 9-cm loaf pan, a 20-cm ovenproof dish and four 10-cm tart cases. A large, flat 27 x 20-cm tray may also be useful (for toasting almonds and oats, for instance).

 **Blender** – This is a key piece of equipment for making smoothies.

 **Cooling rack** – This will ensure that your cakes, loafs and tarts can cool down with air circulating around them, and will help you to avoid soggy bottoms!

 **Electric mixer or standing mixer** – This helps to speed up the mixing of ingredients, although in most cases you can do it by hand, too.

 **Food processor** – This is a frequently used piece of equipment in this book, as it's used for blending nuts and fruit.

**Measuring spoons** – These allow you to measure accurately small quantities of ingredients, such as baking powder, spices, vinegar and oils.

 **Mixing bowls** – At least one large mixing bowl is needed for the recipes in this book, and you may find it useful to have a few in other sizes, too.

 **Muffin and cupcake cases** – You will need a supply of muffin and cupcake cases for a few of the recipes in this book.

 **Piping bags** – You can buy reusable piping bags online or from supermarkets, or make your own from baking paper.

 **Reusable ice-lolly mould** – For our ice pops recipe (p.97), we recommend a reusable set of lolly moulds that come with lids/sticks. These can be purchased online or at supermarkets.

 **Rolling pin** – This will be useful for rolling out pastry, but if you don't have one, an empty wine bottle will work as a substitute.

 **Scales** – These help your baking to be as accurate as possible. However, if you prefer to use cups, use the conversion chart on the next page.

 **Sieve** – This is a baking essential for aerating dry ingredients. However, if you don't have one, stir dry ingredients (a bowl of flour, salt and baking powder, for instance) with a whisk to get air into the mixture.

# CONVERSIONS AND MEASUREMENTS

All the conversions in the tables below are close approximates, which have been rounded up or down. When using a recipe, always stick to one unit of measurement and do not alternate between them.

**Liquid measurements**
6 ml = 1 tsp
15 ml = 1 tbsp
30 ml = ⅛ cup
60 ml = ¼ cup
120 ml = ½ cup
240 ml = 1 cup
2 tbsp liquid egg white
   = 1 large egg white

**Butter measurements**
30 g = ⅛ cup
55 g = ¼ cup
75 g = ⅓ cup
115 g = ½ cup
150 g = ⅔ cup
170 g = ¾ cup
225 g = 1 cup

**Dried ingredient measurements**
5 g = 1 tsp
15 g = 1 tbsp
150 g flour = 1 cup
225 g caster sugar
   = 1 cup
115 g icing sugar
   = 1 cup
175 g brown sugar
   = 1 cup
200 g sprinkles = 1 cup

# DIETARY REQUIREMENTS

Many of the recipes in this book are suitable for those on a vegan or gluten-free diet. These recipes are indicated with the icons below:

**VE** **Vegan**

**GF** **Gluten free**

All instances of non-dairy milk, yoghurt and chocolate that are given in this book can also be switched to dairy equivalents.

# BREAKFAST BITES AND MORNING PICK-ME-UPS

Coconut, date and banana energy balls
• Fluffy banana and walnut pancakes •
Berry smoothie bowl with cashews and
banana • Chocolate and banana smoothie
bowl • Nutty banana muesli • Banana and
berry oatmeal • Creamy almond toast
with banana pennies • Nutty banana
balls • Date and walnut energy bars •
Chocolate and banana French toast •
Banana-chocolate bites • Banana chips

# COCONUT, DATE AND BANANA ENERGY BALLS

These delicious energy balls are the perfect snack for when you're out and about, or they make a great, quick breakfast if prepared in advance.

## METHOD

Soak the dates in lukewarm water for 30 minutes if they're not already soft.

In a food processer, blitz the cashew nuts, then add the oats and blend again to combine. Add the banana, drained dates, salt and vanilla extract and blend until the mixture comes together. It should be pliant enough to roll into balls.

Take the mixture a heaped teaspoon at a time and roll it into balls. If it's too sticky, put the mix back in the food processor and add more oats. If it's too dry, add a drop of water and blitz.

Roll the energy balls in the shredded coconut to finish and keep refrigerated for up to a week.

**MAKES**

approx. 15 balls

**INGREDIENTS**

8 soft pitted dates (approx. 200 g)
55 g cashew nuts
50 g oats
1 medium, overripe banana
Pinch of salt
½ tsp vanilla extract
50 g shredded coconut

# FLUFFY BANANA & WALNUT PANCAKES

Pancakes were made for long mornings and lazy Sundays. This simple recipe makes it easier than ever to enjoy your favourite breakfast treat.

## METHOD

With a fork, mash the bananas in a bowl until smooth. Add the eggs and whisk until fully incorporated.

Add in the flour and whisk again until combined.

Stir in the walnuts, nutmeg, cinnamon and salt.

Heat the butter in a pan over a medium heat. Once it is hot, pour 2–3 tbsp batter into the pan and let it cook for 30 seconds to a minute. Then flip it over and cook the other side for another 30 seconds, or until the pancake is golden brown.

Transfer onto a plate and set aside in a warm oven while you cook the other pancakes.

Serve the pancakes in a stack and top with chopped walnuts, the banana slices and syrup.

## MAKES

approx. 6 pancakes

## INGREDIENTS

**For the pancakes:**
2 large, overripe
  bananas
2 medium eggs
40 g self-raising flour
20 g walnuts,
  finely chopped
Pinch of nutmeg
½ tsp cinnamon
Pinch of salt
1 tbsp butter

**To serve:**
Chopped walnuts
Handful of
  banana slices
Syrup of choice

# BERRY SMOOTHIE BOWL WITH CASHEWS AND BANANA

This colourful dish is like eating dessert for breakfast, only it's healthy and packed with fruit!

## METHOD

Add the banana, raspberries, blackberries and yoghurt to a blender and blitz until smooth. If you would like a thinner consistency, add a splash of almond milk and mix again.

Pour the smoothie into a bowl and top with cashews, banana slices and chia seeds.

**INGREDIENTS**

**For the smoothie:**
1 large, ripe banana, frozen
80 g frozen raspberries
80 g frozen blackberries
3 heaped tbsp non-dairy plain yoghurt
Splash of almond milk (optional)

**For the toppings:**
20 g cashews
½ banana, sliced
1 tbsp chia seeds

# CHOCOLATE AND BANANA SMOOTHIE BOWL

This decadent breakfast smoothie bowl is the perfect way to welcome the day.

## METHOD

Put the bananas, cocoa powder, yoghurt, milk and vanilla into a blender and blitz until smooth.

Pour the smoothie into a bowl and top with the banana, almonds, macadamia nuts, coconut, chocolate chips and chia seeds.

**SERVES**

1

**INGREDIENTS**

**For the smoothie:**

2 large, overripe
    bananas, frozen
2 tbsp cocoa powder
3 tbsp dairy-free
    plain yoghurt
100 ml almond milk
¼ tsp vanilla extract

**For the toppings:**

½ ripe banana, sliced
20 g almonds
20 g macadamia nuts
1 tbsp shredded
    coconut
1 tsp dairy-free
    chocolate chips
1 tsp chia seeds

# NUTTY BANANA MUESLI

This simple recipe is a nutritional powerhouse bursting with protein and fibre to keep you feeling full until lunchtime.

## METHOD

Heat oven to 180°C/357°F/gas mark 4. Spread out the almonds (reserving 1 tbsp) and oats on a baking tray and toast them in the oven for 8–10 minutes.

Put the oats and almonds in a bowl and mix with the walnuts, cranberries, sunflower seeds and 2 tbsp of the puffed rice. Stir briefly to combine.

To assemble, layer the yoghurt and oat mixture in a bowl or glass. Top with banana slices and the remaining chopped almonds and puffed rice.

## SERVES

1

## INGREDIENTS

15 g plus 1 tbsp
    chopped almonds
40 g oats
3–4 walnuts,
    finely chopped
15 g dried cranberries
1 tbsp sunflower seeds
3 tbsp puffed rice
100 g non-dairy
    plain yoghurt
½ medium, ripe
    banana, sliced

# BANANA AND BERRY OATMEAL

This breakfast is quick, easy and comforting – perfect for kicking off cold winter mornings.

## METHOD

Mash the banana in a bowl with a fork.

Add the banana to a small pan along with the oats, milk and salt.

Heat gently on a medium heat, stirring occasionally, until the mixture thickens and starts to bubble.

Transfer to a bowl and top with the banana slices, almonds, blueberries and coconut.

## SERVES

1

## INGREDIENTS

**For the oatmeal:**
1 medium, overripe banana
45 g oats
250 ml non-dairy milk
Pinch of salt

**For the toppings:**
½ medium, ripe banana, sliced
20 g almonds
20 g blueberries
1 tsp shredded coconut

# CREAMY ALMOND TOAST WITH BANANA PENNIES

Simple and sweet is the name of the game with this delicious breakfast idea.

## METHOD

Put the bread in the toaster or under a grill. While it's toasting, slice the banana.

Once the toast is done, spread each slice with a layer of cream cheese.

Top with the banana, honey and almonds.

1

### INGREDIENTS

2 slices of brown bread
1 large, ripe banana
30 g cream cheese
2 tbsp honey
30 g almonds, broken into pieces

# NUTTY BANANA BALLS

Enjoy almonds, cashews and peanuts in these tasty, nutty bites, which are packed with protein.

## METHOD

If they're not already soft, soak the dates in lukewarm water for 30 minutes, then drain.

In a food processer, blitz the cashew nuts and walnuts. Then add the ground almonds, banana, salt, peanut butter and dates (drained) and blend until the mixture comes together. It should be pliant enough to roll into balls.

Take the mixture a heaped teaspoon at a time and roll it into balls. If it's too sticky, put the mix back in the food processor and add more ground almonds. If it's too dry, add a drop of water and blitz.

Coat the energy balls in the granola to finish, and keep refrigerated for up to a week.

**MAKES**

approx. 15 energy balls

**INGREDIENTS**

8 soft pitted dates
   (approx. 200 g)
55 g cashew nuts
20 g walnuts
50 g ground almonds
1 small, overripe
   banana
Pinch of salt
1 heaped tsp
   peanut butter
50 g granola

# DATE AND WALNUT ENERGY BARS

**MAKES**

12–16 bars

These are the ideal grab-and-go breakfast, with no cooking required!

## METHOD

Line a 20-cm square baking tray with baking paper. If the dates are not already soft, soak them in lukewarm water for 30 minutes, then drain.

Place the walnuts and almonds in a food processor and blend until chopped into tiny pieces. Then add the remaining ingredients and blend until the mixture is paste-like and mixed well.

If the mixture is not already coming together, add water half a tablespoon at a time until it does.

Transfer the mixture to the prepared tin, and press it down into a compact layer using the back of a spoon. Refrigerate for 3 hours, or overnight, then cut into pieces as desired.

Store in an airtight container in a cool, dry place for up to 3 weeks.

## INGREDIENTS

300 g soft pitted dates
180 g walnuts
50 g almonds
1 large, overripe banana
2 tbsp cocoa powder
½ tsp nutmeg
Pinch of salt
1 tbsp vanilla extract

# CHOCOLATE AND BANANA FRENCH TOAST

Enjoy your continental breakfast with extra banana and chocolate!

## METHOD

Whisk the eggs, milk, cinnamon, vanilla and salt in a large bowl until fully incorporated.

Take two slices of bread and make a sandwich with a third of the banana slices and chocolate pieces as a filling. Dip the sandwich in the egg mixture, making sure both sides are well soaked.

Melt the butter in a frying pan over a medium heat. Add the sandwich to the pan, and fry for a couple of minutes on each side, until it is golden brown and the chocolate has begun to melt. Repeat for the other two sandwiches.

Serve straight away.

## SERVES

3

## INGREDIENTS

2 medium eggs
150 ml milk
½ tsp cinnamon
½ tsp vanilla extract
Pinch of salt
6 thick slices
    white bread
2 medium, ripe
    bananas, sliced
120 g dark or milk
    chocolate, chopped
Knob of butter

# BANANA-CHOCOLATE BITES

These energy balls are rich, gooey, chocolatey – and healthy!

## METHOD

If they're not already soft, soak the dates in lukewarm water for 30 minutes, then drain.

In a food processor, blitz the cashew nuts. Then add the oats, banana, dates, salt, vanilla extract and cocoa and blend until the mixture comes together. It should be pliant enough to roll into balls. Then stir in the chocolate chips by hand.

Take the mixture a heaped teaspoon at a time and roll it into balls. If it's too sticky, put the mix back in the food processor and add more oats. If it's too dry, add a drop of water and blitz.

Roll the energy balls in the shredded coconut to finish. Keep refrigerated for up to a week.

## MAKES

approx. 15 energy balls

## INGREDIENTS

10 soft pitted dates
 (approx. 250 g)
55 g cashew nuts
50 g oats
1 small, overripe
 banana
Pinch of salt
1 tsp vanilla extract
1 tbsp cocoa
2 tbsp dairy-free
 chocolate chips
50 g shredded coconut
 (optional)

# BANANA CHIPS

Enjoy these chips on their own, or add them to other dishes, such as muesli, for extra crunch and flavour.

## METHOD

Preheat the oven to 100°C/230°F/gas mark ¼.

Slice the banana thinly – aim for slices to be no thicker than half a centimetre. Place them in a bowl with the lemon juice and mix until the slices are coated.

Line a large tray with baking paper and add the banana slices. They should be spread out and not touching each other.

Bake for an hour, then turn the slices over and bake for another hour. The chips should be golden around the edges, but they will not be crisp at this stage.

Once done remove from the oven and leave them to cool. They should crisp up as they cool.

Eat on the same day, or store in an airtight container in a cool, dry place for up to 3 weeks.

## SERVES

2

## INGREDIENTS

2 large, ripe bananas
Juice of 1 lemon

# CUPCAKES AND MUFFINS

Banana and chocolate chip muffins
• Vegan chocolate cupcakes • Matcha and
banana cupcakes with caramelised peanuts
• Oaty banana muffins • Banana buttercream
icing • Gooey chocolate brownies

# BANANA & CHOCOLATE CHIP MUFFINS

The combination of chocolate and banana is hard to beat – here's a recipe for the tried-and-tested favourite that's sure to go down a treat.

## METHOD

Preheat the oven to 180°C/357°F/gas mark 4 and line a 12-hole muffin tray with cases.

In a large bowl, mash the bananas with a fork until fairly smooth. Then add in the sugars, egg and melted butter, and whisk until combined.

Using a sieve, sift the flour, baking powder, bicarbonate of soda and salt into the bowl and stir with a wooden spoon to combine.

Fold in the chocolate chips and orange zest, and mix well.

Divide the mixture between the muffin cases and top with the banana slices (1–2 per cupcake).

Bake for 15 minutes, or until the muffins are golden on the top, and a skewer comes out clean.

Allow to cool before serving. Store in an airtight container for up to a week.

## MAKES

10 muffins

## INGREDIENTS

2 large, overripe bananas
100 g caster sugar
50 g light brown sugar
1 egg
60 g butter, melted
200 g self-raising flour
½ tsp baking powder
1 tsp bicarbonate of soda
½ tsp salt
50 g chocolate chips
Zest of 1 orange
12–20 banana slices

# VEGAN CHOCOLATE CUPCAKES

There's no dairy in sight with these cupcakes, but they are still creamy and rich.

## METHOD

Preheat the oven to 180°C/357°F/gas mark 4 and line a 12-hole muffin tin with cases. Mash the bananas in a large bowl. Then add the coconut oil, almond milk, vinegar, vanilla extract and sugar, and mix thoroughly to combine.

Using a sieve, sift in the flour, baking powder, bicarbonate of soda, cocoa powder and salt. Stir well until everything is combined. Then fold in the chocolate chips.

Bake for 15–20 minutes, or until a skewer comes out clean, then transfer to a rack and allow to cool.

## MAKES

10–12 cupcakes

## INGREDIENTS

2 large, overripe
    bananas
2 tbsp melted
    coconut oil
120 ml almond milk
1 tsp apple cider
    vinegar
1 tsp vanilla extract
150 g caster sugar
225 g plain flour
1 tsp baking powder
¾ tsp bicarbonate
    of soda
3 tbsp cocoa powder
Pinch of salt
75 g dairy-free
    chocolate chips

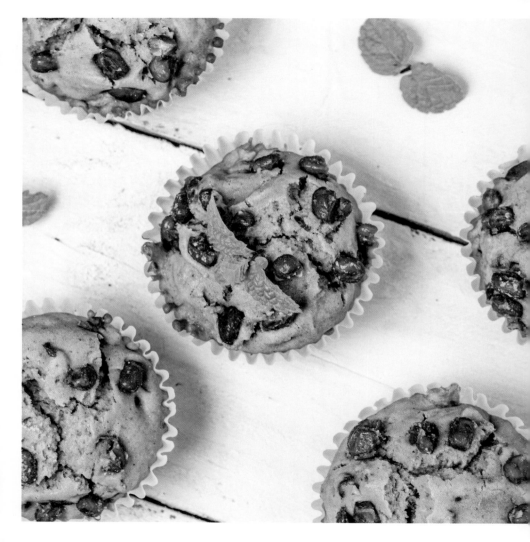

# MATCHA AND BANANA CUPCAKES WITH CARAMELISED PEANUTS

Packed with antioxidants and vitamins, matcha is truly one of the world's superfoods. Add it into these muffins along with caramelised peanuts for a healthy kick to a delicious treat.

## METHOD

Preheat the oven to 180°C/357°F/gas mark 4 and line a 12-hole muffin tray with cases.

In a large bowl, mash the bananas with a fork until smooth. Add in both sugars, the egg and melted butter, and whisk until combined.

Using a sieve, sift the flour, baking powder, bicarbonate of soda, salt and matcha powder into the bowl and stir with a wooden spoon to combine.

Fold in the caramelised peanuts and mix until they are evenly distributed.

Divide the mixture between the muffin cases and bake for 15 minutes, or until a skewer comes out clean.

Allow to cool before serving. Store in an airtight container for up to a week.

**MAKES**

10 cupcakes

**INGREDIENTS**

2 large, overripe
   bananas
70 g caster sugar
50 g light brown sugar
1 egg
60 g butter, melted
200 g self-raising flour
½ tsp baking powder
1 tsp bicarbonate
   of soda
½ tsp salt
1 tbsp matcha powder
70 g caramelised
   peanuts

# OATY BANANA MUFFINS

Whether you're looking for a snack, breakfast or dessert, these oaty banana muffins have you covered.

## METHOD

Preheat the oven to 180°C/357°F/gas mark 4 and line a 12-hole muffin tray with cases.

In a large bowl, mash the bananas with a fork until smooth. Add in both sugars, the egg, melted butter, vanilla extract and milk, and whisk until combined.

Using a sieve, sift the flour, baking powder, bicarbonate of soda and salt into the bowl and stir with a wooden spoon until incorporated. Fold in the oats until combined.

Divide the mixture between the muffin cases and sprinkle a few oats over the top of each one. Bake for 15 minutes, or until a skewer comes out clean.

Allow to cool before serving. Store in an airtight container for up to a week.

## MAKES

10 muffins

## INGREDIENTS

2 large, overripe bananas
50 g caster sugar
50 g light brown sugar
1 egg
100 g butter, melted
½ tsp vanilla extract
130 ml milk
175 g self-raising flour
½ tsp baking powder
1 tsp bicarbonate of soda
½ tsp salt
90 g porridge oats (plus 2 tbsp extra)

# BANANA BUTTERCREAM ICING

Bring banana to any cake or cupcake with this easy buttercream icing.

## METHOD

Mash the banana by hand, or puree it in a food processor, with the aim of getting it as smooth as possible.

Transfer to a large bowl, add the lemon juice and stir well. Then add the butter and beat this into the banana with an electric mixer.

Add the sugar 100 grams at a time, stirring it in a little by hand before mixing with the electric mixer. When the icing is ready it should be a spreadable consistency and hold its shape. If your icing reaches this stage before you've added all the sugar, stop. If your icing is too stiff, add lemon juice a drop or two at a time and mix until you reach the desired consistency.

Spread the icing on cupcakes or a large cake, or keep refrigerated in an airtight container for up to a week.

## MAKES

enough for 10–12 cupcakes

## INGREDIENTS

1 medium, overripe banana
½ tsp lemon juice
80 g non-dairy butter, room temperature
400 g icing sugar

# GOOEY CHOCOLATE BROWNIES

In this recipe, banana is the magic ingredient that allows the classic brownie to become dairy-free.

**METHOD**

Preheat the oven to 180°C/357°F/gas mark 4 and line a 20-cm square tray with baking paper.

In a large bowl, mash the bananas until smooth. Add the sugars and combine with an electric mixer. Then add the almond milk and vegetable oil and mix again.

Put the coffee granules in a cup and dissolve them with 1 tbsp boiling water. Add to the banana mixture and whisk to combine.

Using a sieve, sift in the flour, cocoa powder, salt and baking powder. Fold this into the mixture by hand, until everything is incorporated.

Transfer mixture to the prepared tray and bake for 15 minutes, or until a skewer comes out clean. Remove from the oven and allow to cool in the tin for a few minutes before transferring to a cooling rack. Cut into 12 or 16 squares, depending on how big you would like them to be.

Store in an airtight container for up to 2 weeks.

**MAKES**

12–16 brownies

**INGREDIENTS**

2 large, overripe
    bananas
100 g caster sugar
100 g light
    brown sugar
100 ml almond milk
60 ml vegetable oil
1 tsp instant
    coffee granules
250 g self-raising flour
75 g cocoa powder
1 tsp salt
1 tsp baking powder

# SMOOTHIES AND SHAKES

Chocolate and banana milkshake • Apple and cinnamon shake • Avocado and banana smoothie • Super-green smoothie • Granola-topped berry smoothie • Peanut butter and banana milkshake • Banana oat smoothie • Banana iced coffee

# CHOCOLATE AND BANANA MILKSHAKE

This smoothie is simple but indulgent – ideal for a weekend treat.

## METHOD

Place the banana, chocolate-flavoured milk, cocoa powder and ice cubes into a blender and blitz to combine.

If you prefer your smoothie to be sweeter, add agave syrup a teaspoonful at a time until you reach the desired sweetness.

Transfer to a tall glass and serve immediately, topped with chocolate shavings if desired.

## SERVES

1

## INGREDIENTS

1 large, overripe banana

200 ml chocolate-flavoured soy/almond milk

1 tbsp cocoa powder

3 ice cubes

Agave syrup, to taste (optional)

Non-dairy chocolate shavings, to serve (optional)

# APPLE AND CINNAMON SHAKE

A dash of cinnamon makes this smoothie the perfect autumnal refreshment.

## METHOD

Core and chop the apple into chunks (but keep the peel on) and slice the banana. If the dates are not already soft, soak them in lukewarm water for 30 minutes, then drain.

Add the chopped fruit to a blender along with the dates, vanilla, milk, apple juice, cinnamon, almonds, yoghurt and ice cubes.

Blend until completely smooth and transfer to a glass. If desired, garnish with cinnamon. Serve immediately.

## SERVES

1

## INGREDIENTS

1 large apple

1 large, overripe banana

3 soft pitted dates

½ tsp vanilla extract

150 ml non-dairy milk

50 ml apple juice

1 tsp ground cinnamon (plus optional extra for garnish)

15 g almonds

2 tbsp non-dairy plain yoghurt

3 ice cubes

# AVOCADO AND BANANA SMOOTHIE

Packed with the goodness of avocado and banana, this smoothie will fill you to the brim with get-up-and-go!

### METHOD

Slice the banana, then add to a blender, along with the avocado and all the other ingredients and blitz until smooth.

Transfer to a glass and serve immediately.

**SERVES**

1

**INGREDIENTS**

1 small, overripe
    banana
Flesh of 1 avocado
1 tsp lemon juice
1 tsp agave syrup
½ tsp vanilla extract
200 ml almond milk
3 ice cubes

# SUPER-GREEN SMOOTHIE

Get your greens with this superfood smoothie!

## METHOD

Slice the bananas, then add to a blender along with all the other ingredients. Blitz until smooth.

Transfer to two glasses and serve immediately, topped with extra chia seeds if desired.

## SERVES

2

## INGREDIENTS

2 small, overripe
    bananas
40 g spinach
Flesh of 1 avocado
2 tsp chia seeds,
    plus extra to serve
Flesh of 2 kiwis
400 ml almond milk
6 ice cubes

# GRANOLA-TOPPED BERRY SMOOTHIE

Combine two delicious breakfast varieties in one with this granola-topped smoothie, and get the best of both worlds!

## METHOD

To make the granola, preheat the oven to 140°C/284°F/ gas mark 1. Spread the oats out on a baking tray lined with baking paper and toast them in the oven for 10 minutes. Then remove and wait for them to cool to room temperature.

Melt the coconut oil in a pan over a medium heat, then add one tablespoon of agave nectar and the nutmeg and mix. Add the oats to the coconut-oil mixture and stir until they are coated.

Place the oats back on the tray and toast them in the oven for 3 minutes. Remove from the oven and allow to cool. The granola can be stored in an airtight container at room temperature for up to 3 weeks.

To make the smoothie, place the yoghurt, strawberries, banana, raspberries, oat milk and ice cubes into a blender and blitz until smooth. Add more milk if the smoothie is too thick.

Decant into a glass and sprinkle a handful of granola on top of the smoothie. Add dried fruit for extra flavour if desired. Serve immediately.

**SERVES**

1 (plus extra granola)

**INGREDIENTS**

### For the granola:

50 g oats

1 tsp coconut oil

1 tbsp agave nectar (plus extra to taste)

Pinch of nutmeg

### For the smoothie:

1 tbsp non-dairy plain yoghurt

40 g strawberries, hulled

1 medium, overripe banana

40 g raspberries

150 ml oat milk

3 ice cubes

Dried fruit (optional)

# PEANUT BUTTER AND BANANA MILKSHAKE

**SERVES**

1

With its sweet, nutty flavour, this milkshake is sure to become a favourite.

## METHOD

Place the banana, milk, peanut butter and ice cubes into a blender and blitz to combine.

If you prefer your milkshake to be sweeter, add agave syrup a teaspoonful at a time until you reach the desired sweetness.

Transfer to a glass and add a drizzle of peanut butter and a handful of chopped peanuts to garnish, if desired. Serve immediately.

**INGREDIENTS**

1 large, overripe banana

200 ml unsweetened almond milk

2 heaped tbsp peanut butter

3 ice cubes

Agave syrup, to taste (optional)

Chopped peanuts, to garnish (optional)

Peanut butter, to garnish (optional)

# BANANA OAT SMOOTHIE

This recipe transforms humble ingredients into a creamy and comforting smoothie.

## METHOD

Place the banana, milk, oats, ice cubes and mixed spice into a blender and blitz to combine.

If you prefer your smoothie to be sweeter, add agave syrup a teaspoonful at a time until you reach the desired sweetness.

Transfer to a glass and top with a handful of lightly toasted oats to garnish, if desired. Serve immediately.

**SERVES**

1

**INGREDIENTS**

1 large, overripe banana
200 ml oat milk
3 tbsp rolled oats
3 ice cubes
½ tsp mixed spice
Agave syrup, to taste (optional)
Toasted oats, to garnish (optional)

# BANANA ICED COFFEE

Give a caffeine kick to a traditional smoothie with this simple recipe.

## METHOD

In a blender, combine all ingredients until smooth. Adjust the consistency to your liking by adding more milk or ice cubes.

Transfer to a glass and top with extra coffee beans and cinnamon if desired. Serve immediately.

## SERVES

1

## INGREDIENTS

30 ml espresso,
    or strong coffee, cold
1 small, overripe
    banana
70 ml non-dairy milk
1 tbsp maple syrup
¼ tsp cinnamon, plus
    extra for dusting
    (optional)
3 ice cubes
Coffee beans (optional)

# SWEET
# TREATS

Banana and cinnamon buns • Pumpkin
and sunflower seed cookies • Pan-fried
bananas with salted caramel sauce
• Battered bananas with coconut •
Banana bread • Banana and cherry-
jam crepes • Banana and chocolate tart
• Banoffee millionaire's shortbread

69

# BANANA AND CINNAMON BUNS

There's not much you can do to improve on the classic cinnamon roll – except perhaps by adding banana!

## METHOD

Line a 20-cm square tray with baking paper. To make the filling, mash the banana until smooth, then mix it with the butter. In a separate bowl, add the cinnamon, cocoa powder, sugar and salt. Stir briefly to mix.

Roll out the pastry on a floured surface to a roughly 35 x 20-cm rectangle. Spread the banana mixture evenly over it, then add a layer of the cinnamon mix. Top with the chocolate chips. Then roll up the pastry from the long side. Slice the roll into nine equal parts and place each one on the prepared tray, with a swirl facing up. Cover the tray loosely with foil, and leave for an hour in a warm place to rise.

Preheat the oven to 170°C/338°F/gas mark 3. Remove the foil and bake the rolls for 20–25 minutes, or until they have started to turn golden. If they begin to brown too quickly, then replace the foil loosely over the tray.

While the rolls are baking, make the glaze by mixing the icing sugar and vanilla extract together. Add the milk a few drops at a time until the glaze is smooth and thick. Cover with clingfilm and put to one side.

When the rolls are done, leave them to cool on a rack. When they are cool enough to touch, top with the glaze and serve immediately, or store in an airtight container for up to 5 days.

### MAKES
9 buns

### INGREDIENTS
**For the filling:**
1 medium, overripe banana
30 g unsalted butter, at room temperature
1½ tbsp ground cinnamon
½ tsp cocoa powder
50 g soft brown sugar
Pinch of salt
50 g dark chocolate chips

**For the pastry:**
1 block/sheet puff pastry (approx. 300 g)

**For the glaze:**
150 g icing sugar
1 tsp vanilla extract
1–2 tsp milk

# PUMPKIN & SUNFLOWER SEED COOKIES

Don't be fooled by their size – these little cookies are bursting with energy and goodness.

## METHOD

Soak the dates in lukewarm water for 30 minutes, then drain. Preheat the oven to 150°C/300°F/gas mark 2 and line a 20-cm square tray with baking paper.

Blitz the pumpkin and sunflower seeds to small pieces in a food processor and set aside. In a small cup, add the chia seeds with 3 tbsp cold water. Stir briefly and leave to stand for a few minutes or until the mixture has thickened.

Blitz the banana, drained dates and agave syrup together in a food processor. Transfer to a bowl, then add the seeds and remaining ingredients. Stir until combined. Take a teaspoon of dough and press it into a cookie shape with your hands. Place on the prepared baking tray and repeat until all the dough has been used up.

Bake for 20 minutes, or until the edges of the cookies are starting to turn golden. Allow to cool before serving. Store in an airtight container for up to 2 weeks.

**MAKES**

12–16 cookies

**INGREDIENTS**

6 soft pitted dates
50 g pumpkin seeds
30 g sunflower seeds
1 tbsp ground
  chia seeds
1 large, overripe
  banana
1 tsp agave syrup
70 g oats
50 g raisins
30 g cranberries

# PAN-FRIED BANANAS WITH SALTED CARAMEL SAUCE

This luxurious salted caramel sauce is so creamy you won't believe it's dairy free.

## METHOD

To make the sauce, add the sugar to a pan and heat gently for 2 minutes, stirring occasionally. Then add the coconut milk and bring to the boil, stirring all the time.

Turn the heat down and allow the mixture to simmer for 15–20 minutes. Stir occasionally. When the mixture is sticky and has thickened slightly, remove from the heat and stir in the vanilla and salt. Allow to cool to room temperature before using.

For the bananas, melt the coconut oil in a frying pan over a medium heat. Add the banana slices and cook on each side for 2 minutes.

Transfer to a plate and serve immediately topped with the salted caramel sauce.

**SERVES**

2

**INGREDIENTS**

**For the sauce:**
85 g light brown sugar
115 ml full-fat
    coconut milk
½ tsp vanilla extract
Pinch of salt
    (or more to taste)

**For the bananas:**
2 tsp coconut oil
2 large, overripe
    bananas, sliced

# BATTERED BANANAS WITH COCONUT

This pudding can get messy in the making, but it's worth it for the tasty end result!

## METHOD

Sift the flour, cornflour and salt into a bowl, add the sugar and mix together. In a separate bowl, combine the milk, eggs and coconut extract. Add to the flour mixture and whisk until the batter is smooth.

Cut the bananas in half at the midpoint.

Choose a medium-sized pan with a lid. Pour the oil into the pan and heat it very gradually over a low–medium heat. Test the heat by dropping a tiny bit of batter in. If it sizzles immediately, it's ready.

Dip each piece of banana in the batter, then gently transfer it to the pan with tongs or two forks. Cook on each side for about a minute. Transfer the fried bananas to a piece of kitchen roll to absorb excess oil, then move to a plate.

Dust with icing sugar and chocolate sauce if desired, and serve immediately.

## MAKES

4 battered bananas

## INGREDIENTS

90 g plain flour
30 g cornflour
Pinch of salt
2 tsp caster sugar
70 ml milk
2 small eggs
4 drops coconut extract
4 medium, overripe bananas
400 ml oil

**To serve:**
2 tbsp icing sugar
Chocolate sauce

# BANANA BREAD

Try this recipe for the American classic: banana bread.

## METHOD

Preheat the oven to 180°C/357°F/gas mark 4 and line a 17 x 9 x 9-cm loaf pan with baking paper.

In a large bowl, cream the butter and sugars together until the mixture is light and pale. Then add the eggs, and beat well.

In a separate bowl, sift together the ground almonds, self-raising flour, baking powder and salt. Stir briefly to mix, then add into the egg mixture, and fold it in with a metal spoon. If the mixture is very stiff at this point and difficult to stir, add a tablespoon of milk to loosen it.

Finally, add the mashed bananas into the batter, and stir until well distributed. Pour the mixture into the prepared loaf tin. Slice the remaining banana lengthways down the middle. Place each piece flat side up on the top of the batter.

Bake for 20 minutes, then cover the tin loosely with foil to prevent the top from burning and bake for a further 20–25 minutes, or until a skewer comes out clean. Allow to cool for a few minutes in the tin before transferring to a rack to cool completely. Store in an airtight container for up to a week.

## MAKES

1 loaf

## INGREDIENTS

150 g butter, softened
70 g caster sugar
50 g soft brown sugar
2 eggs, room
    temperature
2 tbsp ground almonds
160 g self-raising flour
1 tsp baking powder
½ tsp salt
1 tbsp milk
2 large, overripe
    bananas, mashed
1 medium,
    overripe banana,
    for decoration

# BANANA AND CHERRY-JAM CREPES

It doesn't have to be Pancake Day – these crepes make a great dessert all year round.

## METHOD

To make the batter, add the flour and salt to a large bowl and stir briefly to combine. In a separate bowl, whisk together the eggs and milk. Once combined, add to the flour and whisk until the batter is smooth.

Add a small knob of butter to a frying pan and put over a medium heat. Once the butter has melted, spoon some of the batter into the pan and quickly spread it so the pan base is thinly coated. Cook for about a minute, until the bottom of the crepe is golden brown, then flip and cook the other side for another minute. Transfer onto a plate and set aside in a warm oven while you cook the other crepes.

To assemble, spread a thin layer of cherry jam on the crepes, add a few banana slices to each and finish with a quick drizzle of lemon juice and some chocolate sprinkles. Then fold the crepes as desired and serve immediately.

## MAKES

10–12 crepes

## INGREDIENTS

**For the crepes:**
150 g plain flour
½ tsp salt
3 eggs
375 ml milk
Knob of butter,
   for frying

**For the filling:**
Jar of smooth
   cherry jam
4 large, overripe
   bananas, sliced
1 lemon, cut into
   small wedges
Chocolate sprinkles

# BANANA AND CHOCOLATE TART

This fancy dessert is, in fact, very simple to make (but don't let on to your friends!).

## METHOD

To make the chocolate ganache filling, chop the chocolate into small pieces, transfer to a heatproof bowl and set aside. Put the cream and sugar in a pan over a medium heat, and stir gently until it's just below boiling point (it will be steaming, and tiny bubbles will appear around the edge of the pan). Pour the cream slowly over the chocolate, and leave it for 2 minutes. Then mix the ganache with a whisk or metal spoon until it becomes smooth and glossy. Add the butter and salt and keep whisking until the butter has melted.

Layer the bottom of each tartlet with the banana slices. Divide the ganache between the two tarts, filling each one to the brim. Refrigerate for at least an hour to set the ganache.

For the decorations, use a vegetable peeler to peel shavings off the white chocolate. When the ganache has set, sprinkle the white chocolate curls around the edge of each tart, and top with banana chips if desired.

## MAKES

2 tarts

## INGREDIENTS

**For the pastry:**
2 medium
   pastry tartlets

**For the filling:**
150 g dark chocolate
150 ml double cream
1 tsp caster sugar
20 g butter,
   in small chunks
Pinch of salt
1 medium, overripe
   banana, sliced

**For the decorations:**
White chocolate,
   room temperature
   (optional)
Dried banana chips
   (optional)

# BANOFFEE MILLIONAIRE'S SHORTBREAD

Make your friends and family feel like a million dollars with this luxurious treat.

## METHOD

Line a 20-cm square tin with baking paper. To make the shortbread, in a large bowl, cream the butter and sugar together until light and fluffy. Sift in the flour and salt and stir until you have a smooth dough. Press the dough into the bottom of the baking tray, prick the top lightly with a fork, and refrigerate for an hour.

Preheat the oven to 180°C/357°F/gas mark 4 and bake the shortbread for 15–20 minutes, or until the top begins to turn golden. Leave in the tin to cool. To make the banana caramel, puree the banana in a food processor, then sieve it to remove any lumps, helping the mixture through with the back of a spoon. Combine the coconut milk, sugars and vanilla in a pan, slowly bring to the boil and keep it bubbling over a medium heat for a few minutes, stirring continuously until the caramel thickens. Then stir in the banana, and leave to cool for a few minutes. Spread the caramel over the shortbread and refrigerate for an hour, or until set.

Melt the dark chocolate in a bowl over a pan of simmering water. Stir occasionally. Once melted, spread over the top of the set caramel layer. Use a knife or spatula to make it smooth. Refrigerate until set, then remove from the tin, slice and serve. Store in an airtight container for up to a week.

**MAKES**

10–12 squares

**INGREDIENTS**

**For the shortbread:**
190 g non-dairy butter
85 g caster sugar
220 g plain flour
Pinch of salt

**For the caramel:**
1 small, overripe
   banana
200 ml full-fat
   coconut milk
60 g light brown sugar
30 g caster sugar
½ tsp vanilla extract

**For the topping:**
350 g non-dairy dark
   chocolate, chopped

# FROZEN SWEETS

Miracle banana ice cream
• Banana, cashew and chocolate ice cream
• Mint choc-chip banana ice cream
• Summer strawberry and banana sorbet
• Chocolate fudge ice lollies • Banana lollies
• Cherry and banana ice-cream sandwiches

# MIRACLE BANANA ICE CREAM

You'll be hard-pressed to find a recipe simpler than this one-ingredient wonder!

## METHOD

Peel and roughly slice the bananas, and place in an airtight, freezer-safe container. Freeze the bananas for at least 3 hours, or overnight, or until they are completely frozen.

To make the ice cream, begin by pulsing the frozen banana in a food processor. As it begins to break up, blend continuously until it becomes smooth and thick. You may have to stop and scrape down the sides every now and then.

Once the mixture is smooth, return it to the freezer-safe container and freeze again for a short time until it has set. Then, serve!

This simple recipe can be spiced up any way you want. After the banana has been blended, try mixing in spices such as nutmeg and cinnamon, a handful of your favourite berries, or some nuts such as pistachios or walnuts.

**SERVES**

4

**INGREDIENTS**

4 large, overripe bananas

# BANANA, CASHEW AND CHOCOLATE ICE CREAM

**SERVES**

4

Chocolate, banana and creamy cashews make this ice cream a winner.

## METHOD

Roughly slice the bananas, and place in an airtight, freezer-safe container. Freeze the bananas for at least 3 hours, or overnight, or until they are completely frozen.

While the banana is freezing, soak the cashew nuts in water (ideally overnight).

To make the ice cream, begin by pulsing the frozen banana in a food processor. As it begins to break up, blend continuously until it becomes smooth and thick. You may have to stop and scrape down the sides every now and then.

When the mixture is smooth, drain and add the cashews, and also the cocoa powder. Blend for a further minute until combined.

Return the ice cream to the freezer to set. Serve topped with the walnuts, if desired.

## INGREDIENTS

4 large, overripe bananas

80 g cashew nuts

4 tbsp cocoa powder

**To serve:**

Handful of walnuts, broken into pieces (optional)

# MINT CHOC-CHIP BANANA ICE CREAM

Try this classic flavour with a twist!

## METHOD

Peel and roughly slice the bananas, and place in an airtight, freezer-safe container. Freeze the bananas for at least 3 hours, or overnight, or until they are completely frozen.

To make the ice cream, begin by pulsing the frozen banana in a food processor. As it starts to break up, blend continuously until it becomes smooth and thick. You may have to stop and scrape down the sides every now and then.

When the mixture is smooth, add the peppermint extract and chocolate chips. Blend for a further minute until combined.

Return the ice cream to the freezer in the airtight, freezer-safe container to set. Serve topped with extra chocolate chips, if desired.

## SERVES

4

## INGREDIENTS

4 large, overripe bananas

2 tsp peppermint extract

150 g dairy-free chocolate chips (plus extra to serve)

# SUMMER STRAWBERRY AND BANANA SORBET

Be transported to summertime with this fresh and fruity sorbet.

## METHOD

Peel and roughly slice the bananas, wash and hull the strawberries, and place the fruit in an airtight, freezer-safe container. Freeze for at least 3 hours, or overnight, until it is completely frozen.

To make the ice cream, begin by pulsing the frozen fruit in a food processor. As it begins to break up, blend continuously until it becomes smooth and thick. You may have to stop and scrape down the sides every now and then.

When the mixture is smooth, return it to the freezer in the airtight, freezer-safe container to set. Serve topped with extra strawberries, if desired.

**SERVES**

4

**INGREDIENTS**

4 large, overripe bananas

400 g strawberries (plus extra to serve)

# CHOCOLATE FUDGE ICE LOLLIES

This frozen dessert is a great treat for hot summer days.

## METHOD

Preheat the oven to 180°C/357°F/gas mark 4 and roast the hazelnuts for 5 minutes. Remove the skins, then blitz them in a food processor along with the vegetable oil until they turn into a paste. This should take a few minutes.

Meanwhile, put the dates in a pan with 120 ml water and simmer for 5 minutes, until nearly all the liquid has gone.

Add the bananas, cocoa powder, dates (plus any remaining liquid) and coconut milk to the food processor with the hazelnut paste and blitz until smooth.

Distribute the mixture equally between the ice lolly moulds, add the lolly stick/lid and freeze overnight.

To remove the ice lollies from the moulds, place them in warm water until you can pull the lolly away from the mould.

Eat immediately or store them frozen in an airtight container for up to a month.

**MAKES**

8 ice lollies

**INGREDIENTS**

70 g hazelnuts
1 tsp vegetable oil
80 g soft pitted
    dates, chopped
2 large, overripe
    bananas
2 tbsp cocoa powder
230 ml full-fat
    coconut milk

**EXTRA EQUIPMENT**

8 lolly moulds and
    8 lolly sticks (or a
    reusable ice-lolly
    mould set)

# BANANA LOLLIES

These treats are the banana's answer to the toffee apple.

**METHOD**

Preheat the oven to 120°C/248°F/gas mark ½ and line two large baking trays with baking paper. To make the meringue, put the aquafaba and lemon juice in a bowl, and mix with an electric hand mixer until white, glossy peaks begin to form. This should take a few minutes. Then, add the sugar in gradually, mixing all the time. Continue to whip until the meringue holds stiff peaks. If you would like, add a drop of food colouring to the meringue at this point.

Transfer the meringue to a piping bag, snip off the end and pipe small rounds onto one of the prepared trays. Bake for 45 minutes, then turn the oven off and leave the meringues inside for another hour to dry out. Once done, remove from the oven and allow to cool. Then break them into different-sized pieces.

To make the lollies, chop the bananas in half. Melt the chocolate in a bowl over a pan of simmering water. Skewer the banana halves onto sticks and dip them in the chocolate. Decorate with the crushed meringue pieces while the chocolate is still melted and leave on the other large tray to set. Freeze for at least 30 minutes, and then serve. Store them frozen in an airtight container for up to a month.

**MAKES**

5 lollies

**INGREDIENTS**

**For the meringue:**
100 ml aquafaba
(water from tin
of chickpeas)
¼ tsp lemon juice
100 g caster sugar
Food colouring
(optional)

**For the lollies:**
5 medium, overripe
bananas
200 g non-dairy
milk chocolate

**EXTRA EQUIPMENT**

5 lolly sticks

# CHERRY AND BANANA ICE-CREAM SANDWICHES

What's better than ice cream? Cookies *and* ice cream! We've suggested using cherries, but this recipe works well with any summer fruit.

## METHOD

Roughly slice the bananas, and place in an airtight, freezer-safe container. Freeze the bananas for at least 3 hours, or overnight, or until they are completely frozen.

To make the ice cream, begin by pulsing the frozen banana in a food processor. As it begins to break up, blend continuously until it becomes smooth and thick. You may have to stop and scrape down the sides every now and then.

Once the mixture is smooth, add in the cherries and pulse until they are just beginning to break up. Return the mixture to the freezer-safe container and freeze for a short time until it sets again. Serve the ice cream sandwiched between two cookies.

If you want to take this recipe to the next level, why not try it with the cookies on p.73?

**MAKES**

4 ice-cream sandwiches

**INGREDIENTS**

2 large, overripe bananas
200 g cherries, stoned
8 chocolate chip cookies

# DELICIOUS DESSERTS

Banoffee pie • Banana upside-down cake • Iced banana cake • Apple and banana crumble • No-bake peanut butter cheesecake • Creamy custard tarts • Raw chocolate and walnut tart • No-bake banana cheesecake • Banana, maple and hazelnut semolina pudding • No-bake strawberry and banana cheesecakes

# BANOFFEE PIE

Is there any other pudding quite as distinctive as banoffee pie? Probably not! Here's a simple recipe for this classic 1970s dessert.

## METHOD

Grease a 20-cm square springform tin.

Blitz all the biscuits in a food processor – or crush them with a rolling pin – then add the melted butter and mix again until the biscuits are coated. Pack the crumbs into the bottom of your pan and refrigerate for an hour.

Spread the caramel over the biscuit base, then add a layer of bananas on top.

In a medium bowl whisk the cream until it is thick and light. Spread or pipe over the bananas, then grate the chocolate over the top. Keep refrigerated and consume within 3 days.

## SERVES

10–12

## INGREDIENTS

**For the base:**
Knob of butter,
    for greasing
150 g digestive biscuits
100 g ginger-nut
    biscuits
125 g butter, melted

**For the caramel:**
1 tin caramel
    (approx. 400 g)

**For the topping:**
3 medium, overripe
    bananas, sliced
200 ml whipping
    cream
50 g chocolate
    of choice

# BANANA UPSIDE-DOWN CAKE

Try this twist on the traditional upside-down cake, featuring bananas and a spicy-sweet hint of cardamom.

## METHOD

Preheat the oven to 180°C/357°F/gas mark 4 and line a 20-cm square tin with baking paper.

To make the topping, in a medium bowl, beat the butter and sugar until light and fluffy. Add the cardamom and salt and beat again until mixed. Spread over the bottom of the tin, then arrange the banana lengths, flat side down, over the mixture.

Place the butter, flour, sugars, salt, cardamom, cinnamon and baking powder in a large bowl and mix with an electric mixer until combined. Add the eggs and vanilla and beat well. Layer the mixture on top of the bananas and bake for 25–30 minutes, until a skewer comes out clean. Allow the cake to cool for 30 minutes before turning it out onto a rack. Keep in an airtight container and consume within 1 week.

**SERVES**

10–12

**INGREDIENTS**

**For the topping:**
50 g butter
60 g light brown sugar
½ tsp cardamom
Pinch of salt
9–10 small, overripe bananas, halved lengthways

**For the cake:**
150 g butter, softened
150 g self-raising flour
100 g caster sugar
50 g light brown sugar
Pinch of salt
½ tsp cardamom
½ tsp cinnamon
½ tsp baking powder
2 medium eggs
½ tsp vanilla extract

# ICED BANANA CAKE

This is the perfect coffee-break cake – best enjoyed while you have your feet up!

## METHOD

Preheat the oven to 180°C/357°F/gas mark 4 and grease two 20-cm round cake tins.

In a large bowl, cream the sugar and butter together. Add the banana and beat until incorporated. Sift in the flour, baking powder, baking soda and a pinch of salt and fold in. Then stir in the hazelnuts and vinegar.

Divide the mixture between the two tins and bake for 15 minutes, until a skewer comes out clean. Place on a rack to cool.

To make the icing, beat the butter, sugar and vanilla extract together in a large bowl. If the icing is too stiff to spread, add milk a few drops at a time to soften it.

Sandwich the two cakes together with icing, then cover the whole of the cake with the remaining icing. Decorate with banana chips if desired. Keep in an airtight container and consume within 1 week.

## SERVES

10–12

## INGREDIENTS

**For the cake:**
150 g caster sugar
70 g non-dairy butter, plus extra for greasing
3 large bananas, mashed
270 g self-raising flour
1 tsp baking powder
1 tsp baking soda
Pinch of salt
50 g hazelnuts, chopped
1 tbsp apple cider vinegar

**For the icing:**
170 g non-dairy butter
600 g icing sugar
½ tsp vanilla extract
2 tbsp non-dairy milk

**To decorate:**
Banana chips (see p.35)

# APPLE AND BANANA CRUMBLE

This crumble recipe is easily made dairy- and gluten-free – something that everybody can enjoy.

## METHOD

Preheat the oven to 180°C/357°F/gas mark 4 and grease a 20-cm ovenproof dish.

To make the filling, add the fruit to a large pan along with a tablespoon of water and a tablespoon of the sugar. Cook the fruit uncovered on a low heat for 5 minutes, stirring occasionally, until it has softened a little. Then add the rest of the sugar, the flour, the cinnamon and salt. Stir thoroughly to combine and put to one side.

Meanwhile, put all the topping ingredients into a bowl and rub them together with the tips of your fingers until they resemble breadcrumbs.

Put the fruit mixture into the bottom of the prepared dish, then sprinkle the crumble topping over the fruit evenly.

Bake for 30–40 minutes, until the fruit is bubbling and the top is golden brown. Allow to cool on a cooling rack before serving. Keep refrigerated and consume within 3 days.

**SERVES**
8–10

**INGREDIENTS**

### For the filling:
Knob of non-dairy butter for greasing
300 g cooking apples, peeled and chopped
1 medium banana, lightly mashed
60 g light brown sugar
1 tbsp plain flour (or gluten-free flour)
1 tsp cinnamon
½ tsp salt

### For the topping:
200 g plain flour (or gluten-free flour)
20 g light brown sugar
160 g non-dairy butter
Pinch of salt

# NO-BAKE PEANUT BUTTER CHEESECAKE

There's no cooking required for this rich, nutty cheesecake.

## METHOD

Grease a 20-cm square springform tin.

Blitz the biscuits in a food processor until they are crumbs. Melt the butter, then add to the biscuits, and mix again until combined. Press the biscuit mixture into the tin and refrigerate for an hour.

Puree the bananas in a food processor and strain through a sieve to get rid of any lumps, pushing it through with the back of a spoon if needed. Then add the puree back to the food processor along with the cashew nuts (drained), coconut oil, milk, water, lemon juice and peanut butter. Blitz until smooth. Spread the mixture over the biscuit base and refrigerate for another 2 hours.

Before serving, chop the chocolate into small pieces and melt it in a bowl over a pan of simmering water. Drizzle over the cheesecake and add a sprinkling of peanuts. Keep refrigerated and consume within 3 days.

**SERVES**
8–10

**INGREDIENTS**

**For the biscuit base:**
250 g non-dairy oat biscuits
125 g non-dairy butter,
    plus extra for greasing

**For the filling:**
2 medium, overripe
    bananas
180 g cashew nuts, soaked
    overnight in water
60 g coconut oil
80 ml non-dairy milk
1 tbsp water
Juice of 1 lemon
2 tbsp peanut butter

**For the topping:**
100 g dark chocolate
Peanuts

# CREAMY CUSTARD TARTS

These little tarts are almost too pretty to eat! (Almost...)

## METHOD

Preheat the oven to 180°C/357°F/gas mark 4 and grease and line four 10-cm tart cases. Divide the pastry into four. Roll out one piece to at least a 12-cm circle, press it into the tart case and cut off the excess. Prick the bottom lightly with a fork. Repeat for the other three pieces.

Cover the top of the pastry cases with baking paper and weigh each one down with baking beans or uncooked rice. Bake for 10 minutes. Then remove the paper and beans, and bake for a further 10–15 minutes, or until the pastry is golden. Remove and allow to cool on a rack. Put one of the bananas in a food processor and blend until smooth, then sieve it to remove any lumps, pushing the mixture through with the back of a spoon if needed. Set to one side.

Heat the custard in a small pan, then add the banana puree and banana extract and stir until incorporated. Heat until the custard is steaming. Divide the custard between each tart case, leave to cool for a few minutes, and then refrigerate for an hour. Once the custard is completely cool, slice the second banana and top the tarts with the banana and strawberry slices, and a few mint leaves if desired. Keep refrigerated and consume within 3 days.

## MAKES

4 tarts

## INGREDIENTS

**For the pastry:**
Knob of butter,
    for greasing
240 g sweet
    shortcrust pastry

**For the filling:**
2 large, overripe
    bananas
500 ml vanilla custard
½ tsp banana extract
200 g strawberries,
    sliced
Mint leaves,
    to garnish (optional)

# RAW CHOCOLATE AND WALNUT TART

This smooth and creamy tart is the perfect dessert to round off your meal.

## METHOD

Grease a 20-cm square springform tin. If the dates are not already soft, soak them in lukewarm water for 30 minutes, then drain (the dates for the base and filling can be soaked and drained at the same time).

To make the base, blend the ground almonds, coconut, almond butter, coconut oil and four dates in a food processor until a dough has formed. Press the dough into the tin, so it covers the whole surface, and refrigerate for an hour.

For the filling, blend the remaining dates, banana, coconut oil, salt and cocoa powder until smooth. Stir in the chopped walnuts and spread over the biscuit base. Freeze for 3 hours.

For the topping, melt the chocolate in a bowl over a pan of simmering water. Add the melted coconut oil and stir until combined. Spread the chocolate thinly over the tart while it's still frozen, then refrigerate until the chocolate has set. Bring to room temperature to serve. Keep refrigerated and consume within 3 days.

**SERVES**

8–10

**INGREDIENTS**

### For the base:
Knob of non-dairy butter,
    for greasing
250 g ground almonds
150 g desiccated coconut
4 tbsp almond butter
4 tbsp coconut oil, melted
4 soft pitted dates

### For the filling:
150 g soft pitted dates
1 small, overripe banana
4 tbsp coconut oil, melted
Pinch of salt
½ tbsp cocoa powder
80 g walnuts, chopped

### For the topping:
150 g non-dairy dark chocolate
1 tsp coconut oil, melted

# NO-BAKE BANANA CHEESECAKE

This classic recipe is beautiful on its own, but can be customised with your favourite fruits and sauces.

## METHOD

Grease a 20-cm square springform tin.

Blitz the biscuits in a food processor until they are crumbs. Melt the butter, then add to the biscuits, and mix again until combined. Press the biscuit mixture into the bottom and sides of the tin, and refrigerate for an hour.

Puree the bananas in a food processor and strain through a sieve to get rid of any lumps, pressing it through with the back of a spoon if needed. Then add the puree back to the food processor along with the cashew nuts (drained), sugar, coconut oil, milk, almond butter, banana extract, water and lemon juice. Blitz until smooth. Spread the mixture over the biscuit base and refrigerate for another 2 hours.

Top with your favourite fruit, and serve with caramel sauce if desired. Keep refrigerated and consume within 3 days.

**SERVES**

8–10

**INGREDIENTS**

**For the base:**
250 g non-dairy oat biscuits
125 g non-dairy butter,
    plus extra for greasing

**For the filling:**
2 medium, overripe bananas
180 g cashew nuts, soaked
    overnight in water
50 g icing sugar
60 g coconut oil
80 ml non-dairy milk
1 tbsp almond butter
1 tsp banana extract
1 tbsp water
Juice of 1 lemon

**To serve:**
Fruit
Caramel sauce

# BANANA, MAPLE AND HAZELNUT SEMOLINA PUDDING

This winter warmer is comforting and filling – just the thing for cosy nights in.

## METHOD

Put the milk, semolina, sugar and salt in a saucepan over a medium heat. Stir continuously until the mixture begins to thicken. This should take a few minutes.

Once it's thick, simmer the semolina mixture for 2 minutes, still stirring. Then remove from the heat and stir in the nut butter.

Divide the mixture between four bowls, and top with banana slices, hazelnuts and maple syrup. Serve immediately.

**SERVES**

4

**INGREDIENTS**

500 ml non-dairy milk
40 g fine semolina
2 tsp light brown sugar
Pinch of salt
1 tbsp hazelnut butter
    (or other nut butter)
1 medium, overripe
    banana, sliced
40 g hazelnuts,
    roughly chopped
4 tbsp maple syrup

# NO-BAKE STRAWBERRY & BANANA CHEESECAKES

These beautiful mini cheesecakes pack a fruity flavour punch!

## METHOD

Grease a 12-hole muffin tin. Cut out 24 thin strips of baking paper, each one approximately 15 cm long and 1 cm wide. Take two strips of paper per muffin hole, and place them in a cross shape in the well. The tabs should stick up over the top of the tray and will enable you to pull the cheesecake out easily when it's set.

Blitz the biscuits in a food processor until they are crumbs. Melt the butter, then add to the biscuits, and mix again until combined. Divide the mixture into 12 and press one portion into each hole in the tin. Refrigerate for an hour.

Puree the banana in a food processor and strain through a sieve to get rid of any lumps, using the back of a spoon to push it through. Set to one side. Do the same for the strawberries. Add the cashew nuts (drained), coconut oil, milk, almond butter, water and lemon juice to a food processor and blitz until smooth. Divide the mixture into two. Stir the banana puree into one and the strawberry puree into the other.

Spread the banana mixture over the biscuit bases, filling the wells to about two thirds full. Refrigerate for 30 minutes. Then top up the rest of the wells with the strawberry mixture. Refrigerate for 2 hours.

Serve topped with extra strawberries and a sprig of mint if desired. Keep refrigerated and consume within 3 days.

**MAKES**
12 mini cheesecakes

**INGREDIENTS**

**For the base:**
250 g non-dairy
  oat biscuits
125 g non-dairy butter,
  plus extra for greasing

**For the filling:**
1 medium, overripe
  banana
100 g strawberries,
  plus extra to serve
180 g cashew nuts,
  soaked overnight
  in water
60 g coconut oil
80 ml non-dairy milk
1 tbsp almond butter
1 tbsp water
Juice of 1 lemon
Mint leaves, to garnish

# RECIPE INDEX

# IMAGE CREDITS

If you're interested in finding out more about our books,
find us on Facebook at **Summersdale Publishers** and
follow us on Twitter at **@Summersdale**.


**www.summersdale.com**